INSIDE THE NFL

NFC WEST

THE ARIZONA CARDINALS

THE ST. LOUIS RAMS

THE SAN FRANCISCO 49ERS

THE SEATTLE SEAHAWKS

BY K. C. KELLEY

The Child's World®

Published in the United States of America by
The Child's World® • 1980 Lookout Drive
Mankato, MN 56003-1705

800-599-READ • www.childsworld.com

ACKNOWLEDGEMENTS

The Child's World®: Mary Berendes,
Publishing Director

The Design Lab: Kathleen Petelinsek,
Design; Gregory Lindholm, Page Production

Manuscript consulting and photo research
by Shoreline Publishing Group LLC.

Thanks to John Walters and Jim Gigliotti
for their assistance on this book.

PHOTOS

Cover: Joe Robbins (front and back)
Interior: AP/Wide World: 5, 6, 13, 15, 19,
20, 26, 30, 38; Corbis: 8; Getty Images: 29;
Joe Robbins: 11, 12, 16, 23, 24, 27, 32.

LIBRARY OF CONGRESS
CATALOGING-IN-PUBLICATION DATA

Kelley, K. C.
  NFC West / by K.C. Kelley.
    p. cm. — (Inside the NFL)
  Includes bibliographical references and index.
  ISBN 978-1-60253-000-3
(library bound : alk. paper)
  1. National Football League—History—Juvenile
literature. 2. Football—United States—History—
Juvenile literature. I. Title. II. Series.
  GV955.5.N35K455 2008
  796.332'640973—dc22   2008010518

NFC WEST
INTRODUCTION

T here isn't a more colorful cast of characters in the NFL than those who have played for the teams in the National Football Conference (NFC) West Division. The teams in this division are the Arizona Cardinals, the St. Louis Rams, the San Francisco 49ers, and the Seattle Seahawks.

These clubs have brought us men with names such as "Crazylegs," "Night Train," and "The King"; groups of players known as the "Fearsome Foursome" and the "Million-Dollar Backfield"; memorable plays like the "Alley-Oop Pass" and "The Catch"; and even fans called the "12th Man"—and there's a story behind every one of those nicknames.

We'll get to all those stories when we talk about the teams in the NFC West in the coming pages. Sometimes these teams have been very good, and sometimes they have not. But they have always been very entertaining.

The 49ers have stumbled recently, but they dominated the West for much of the 1980s and 1990s.

CHAPTER ONE
THE ARIZONA CARDINALS

T he Arizona Cardinals are the oldest **franchise** in the National Football League. But their fans are ready for a new beginning. That's because, even though the club dates to before the turn of the century—the 19th century, that is!—the Cardinals have had only occasional success. Recent history, however, suggests that better times may be just around the corner.

The Cardinals' road to the NFC West was a long one. It began more than 100 years ago and two time zones away, in Chicago. The club began as a neighborhood team in that town in 1898, when the city's Morgan Athletic Club began playing football. The story goes that in the early 1900s, owner Chris O'Brien bought some hand-me-down uniforms that already had been used by the University of Chicago. O'Brien had been told that

Elmer Angsman was a star halfback on the Cardinals' 1947 championship team.

he was getting maroon-colored uniforms, but they had faded over time. When he saw them, O'Brien said, "That's not maroon. It's cardinal." And that's how the Cardinals got their name—not after the bird, which is on their helmet, but after the color.

In 1920, O'Brien paid $100 to enter the Cardinals into the brand-new American **Professional** Football Association (APFA). A couple of years later, the league became known as the National Football League (NFL). The Cardinals were known as the Racine Cardinals in their first season in the league, after a street that bordered their home field. By the next year, though, they were called the Chicago Cardinals.

O'Brien then spent $3,000 to obtain star quarterback John "Paddy" Driscoll in 1920. Driscoll may have saved the franchise that year. The APFA had two Chicago teams, the Cardinals and the Tigers. The Cardinals won a key game between the two teams and became the fans' favorite. The Tigers closed down at the end of the season.

In 1921, the Decatur Staleys moved to Chicago, and a new city **rivalry** was born. The following year, the Staleys renamed themselves the Bears.

In 1929, the Bears and Cardinals met on Thanksgiving Day. Cardinals fullback Ernie Nevers scored six touchdowns. He also kicked four extra points, accounting for all of the Cardinals' points in their 40–6 win. That's still the NFL record for most points scored in a game by one player. And it is the oldest individual mark still standing in the NFL's record book.

Jim Hart was a Pro Bowl quarterback four years in a row in the mid-1970s.

The Cardinals and Bears are the only original APFA franchises still in the NFL. But while the Bears have won nine titles, the Cardinals have had little championship experience. In 1925, they were named NFL champions after finishing with a league-best record of 11–2–1 (there were no **playoffs** then). In 1947, the Cardinals won their only NFL Championship Game, defeating the Philadelphia Eagles 28–21. That Cardinals' team featured the "Dream Backfield" of four star players that was anchored by halfback Charley Trippi, a future member of the Pro Football Hall of Fame. Trippi, a **rookie,** signed a four-year **contract** that was worth $100,000—it was the largest contract in football history at the time.

The Cardinals have not won another title since. In fact, they would not even win another **postseason** game at all for 51 years. In the meantime, they moved twice. In 1960, the team moved to St. Louis, where it remained for 28 seasons. In 1988, the team relocated to Phoenix, Arizona. The club was known as the Phoenix Cardinals for several seasons before becoming the Arizona Cardinals in 1994.

While in St. Louis, the Cardinals featured some high-powered offensive teams under coach Don Coryell. "Air Coryell" was operated by quarterback Jim Hart, and it featured skilled running back Terry Metcalf. Kicker Jim Bakken was another star of that **era.**

In 1974, St. Louis fielded one of its best teams. Hart led the NFC in touchdown passes (20). Metcalf led the conference in yards per carry (4.7) and was the NFL's top kick returner. St. Louis finished 10–4, but lost in the first round of the playoffs. The Cardinals were even better in 1975, finishing 11–3. Again they lost in the first round of the playoffs. The Cardinals would make only one postseason appearance for the next 23 years.

Since moving to the Southwest in 1988, the Cardinals have had only one winning season. It came in 1998. Guided by scrambling quarterback Jake "the Snake" Plummer, the Cardinals went 9–7. They beat Dallas in a **wild-card** playoff game for their first postseason win since 1947. The following week, Arizona lost to Minnesota in a divisional playoff game.

When the NFL underwent a major **realignment** in 2002, Arizona moved again. This time, the move was from the NFC East to the NFC West. The change in divisions did not immediately produce a change in the Cardinals' fortunes. Arizona won only 25 games in its five seasons in the West.

Cardinals' fans are confident that 2007, though, was a sign of good things to come. Under new coach Ken Whisenhunt, Arizona won eight games that season and remained in playoff contention for most of the year. Whisenhunt, who was the offensive coordinator for the Pittsburgh Steelers' team that won **Super Bowl** XL in the 2005 season, has some stars to work with on the offensive side of the ball. Larry Fitzgerald and Anquan Boldin form one of the best wide-receiver **tandems** in the league. At quarterback, **veteran** Kurt Warner (a former NFL MVP for the Rams) and young Matt Leinart (a **Heisman Trophy** winner at Southern California in college) give Whisenhunt a couple of different options. Former Colts star Edgerrin James arrived in 2006 to boost the running game.

Head coach Ken Whisenhunt grew up in Augusta, Georgia, where the famous Masters golf tournament is played. When he was a teenager, Whisenhunt worked on the event's huge, hand-operated scoreboard.

Anquan Boldin is one half of a terrific wide-receiver tandem (Larry Fitzgerald is the other half).

Kurt Warner began 2007 as a backup. He showed flashes of his old MVP form, though, after replacing injured starter Matt Leinart.

In February of 2008, Arizona fans watched as the New England Patriots and the New York Giants played in Super Bowl XLII in the Cardinals' sparkling home stadium, which opened in 2006. Those fans hope that it won't be long until they see their own team playing in the NFL's biggest game.

CHAPTER TWO
THE ST. LOUIS RAMS

T he Rams of the late 1990s and early 2000s featured the "Greatest Show on Turf." It was an incredible collection of talent on offense that produced some of the highest-scoring teams in NFL history. But even long before the "Greatest Show on Turf," the Rams were known for their ability to put points on the scoreboard at a rapid rate. Their great offenses carried the club to championships in three different cities: Cleveland, Los Angeles, and St. Louis.

The Rams began as the Cleveland Rams in 1937. The Rams' championship in Cleveland came in their final year there, in 1945, before the move to Los Angeles. Six years later, the Los Angeles Rams were the champions of the NFL. In 1995, the club moved to St. Louis. In their fifth year in their new town, the Rams won the Super Bowl for the first time.

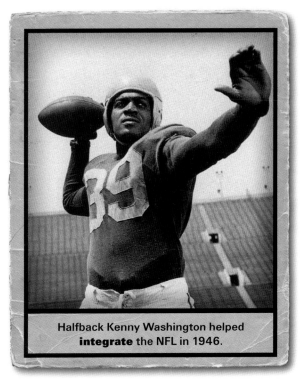

Halfback Kenny Washington helped **integrate** the NFL in 1946.

The common thread on all those teams was great talent on offense. In 1945, for instance, quarterback Bob Waterfield joined the club. In his very first year, Waterfield was named the league's most valuable player. He passed for 1,609 yards and 14 touchdowns (the season was only 10 games long then), and led his team into the NFL Championship Game against the Washington Redskins. On a freezing cold day—it was just 6 degrees (minus-14 C)—Waterfield passed for two touchdowns, and the Rams won 15–14.

The following season, the Rams moved to Los Angeles. They became the first of many pro sports franchises to **migrate** to California. From nearby University of California, Los Angeles (UCLA), they signed Kenny Washington and Woody Strode, the first two African-Americans to play in the NFL since 1933.

Los Angeles embraced its new team. Waterfield, who was young, athletic, and handsome, married a movie star, actress Jane Russell. But the Rams had so many good players on offense that soon another quarterback, Norm Van Brocklin, joined Waterfield on the Rams' roster. It was Van Brocklin's fourth-quarter touchdown pass that lifted the Rams to a 24–17 victory over the Cleveland Browns in the 1951 NFL Championship Game.

The Rams seemed to have as many famous players as the nearby Hollywood studios. Besides Waterfield and Van Brocklin, they featured receivers Elroy "Crazylegs" Hirsch and Tom Fears.

Pro Football Hall of Fame wide receiver Elroy "Crazylegs" Hirsch caught 343 passes for the Rams from 1949 to 1957. His nickname came from the way his legs seemed to go in all different directions when he ran.

Elroy Hirsch shows off the style that earned him the nickname "Crazylegs" in this photo from 1953.

"Crazylegs" was especially popular with fans. As he tried to run off the field after the final game of his career in 1957, he was mobbed. Fans ripped off parts of his uniform for souvenirs.

The Rams were a record-setting machine in the early 1950s. Fears caught 84 passes in 1950, including 18 in a single game. Both were NFL records at the time. Van Brocklin, who shared quarterback duties with Waterfield for a few seasons, passed for an NFL single-game-record 554 yards in a 54–14 defeat of the New York Yanks in 1951.

Roman Gabriel was the Rams' next great quarterback. In 1969, he led Los Angeles to 11 straight wins and was named league MVP.

The heart of the Rams in the 1960s and 1970s, however, was their defensive line. "The Fearsome Foursome," as it was known, consisted of Roosevelt Grier, Deacon Jones, Lamar Lundy, and Merlin Olsen. Those players struck fear in their opponents on the field, although they were gentle giants off the field. Olsen even went on to play the not-so-fearsome Jonathan Garvey in *Little House on the Prairie*, a hit TV series in the 1970s.

The Rams of that era were a model of success and frustration. Los Angeles finished in first place in the NFC West each year from 1973 to 1979. Defensive ends Jack Youngblood and Fred Dryer led a Ram-tough defense that in 1975 allowed only 135 points. That was the second fewest in league history for a 14-game season; NFL teams today play 16 games. The Rams played the Steelers in Super Bowl XIV after the 1979 season. The Rams were a heavy underdog but led in the fourth quarter before losing, 31–19.

In 1984, the Rams moved 50 miles (80.5 kilometers) south to Anaheim (they kept the name Los Angeles). Second-year running back Eric Dickerson ran almost as far. Dickerson, who a year earlier had gained an NFL rookie-record 1,808 yards, this time ran for an NFL single-season-record 2,105 yards.

The Rams moved yet again in 1995. This time, the franchise moved east, to St. Louis. After nine straight losing seasons, the Rams broke out in 1999. First-year starting quarterback Kurt Warner led the franchise to a 13–3 record. Then the Rams, coached by Dick Vermeil, beat the Tennessee Titans 23–16 in Super Bowl XXXIV.

The Rams' offense became known as "The Greatest Show on Turf." Warner was named league MVP in 1999 and in 2001 (a season in which St. Louis went 14–2 under Vermeil's **successor,** Mike Martz). Running back Marshall Faulk was the MVP in 2000, when he scored a then-NFL-record 26 touchdowns.

In the six-season span beginning in 1999, the Rams won three division titles and made the playoffs on two other occasions. They reached the Super Bowl again in 2001, but were upset by the New England Patriots in Super Bowl XXXVI.

By 2004, Warner had left the team, and Faulk began giving way to rookie star Steven Jackson. But with Marc Bulger as quarterback and explosive veterans Torry Holt and Isaac Bruce catching the ball, St. Louis still struck fear in opposing defenses around the league and made the playoffs as a wild-card team.

New coach Scott Linehan took over in 2006. Not surprisingly, offense was the name of the game in his first season in St. Louis. Bulger, Holt, and Jackson all made the Pro Bowl that year. Then, injuries to Bulger and Jackson contributed to a disappointing season in '07. But Rams' fans know that it won't be long before their team is back to putting on an exciting offensive show.

Dick "Night Train" Lane was a star defensive back for the Rams in 1952 and 1953. "Night Train," whose nickname came from a famous song, intercepted 14 passes as a rookie in 1952. That's still an NFL single-season record.

Steven Jackson is a star running back who rushed for more than 1,000 yards for the third **consecutive** year in '07.

CHAPTER THREE

THE SAN FRANCISCO 49ERS

The San Francisco 49ers are best known as the NFL's most powerful **dynasty** of the 1980s. But ever since their first seasons in a rival league in the 1940s, they also have been known as an exciting, high-scoring franchise that has featured lots of colorful characters.

The 49ers were founded in 1946 as part of the All-American Football Conference (AAFC), which competed with the established NFL for fans at the gate and for attention in the newspapers.

The team was coached by local legend Lawrence T. "Buck" Shaw and quarterbacked by hometown favorite Frankie Albert. Joe "The Jet" Perry was a future Pro Football Hall of Fame member at fullback. Perry, the franchise's first African-American player, dashed 58 yards on his first career carry in 1948. In 16 pro seasons, he rushed for 9,723 yards.

Frankie Albert, who later became coach, was the first in a line of star 49ers quarterbacks.

San Francisco rolled through most of the AAFC opponents on its schedule, but could not get past the powerful Cleveland Browns. That team won the league championship all four years of the AAFC's existence.

Still, the 49ers featured many quality players, and fans flocked to Kezar Stadium to watch them play. So in a deal reached late in 1949, San Francisco was one of three AAFC teams (along with Cleveland and Baltimore) that was invited to join the NFL for the 1950 season. As part of the agreement, the AAFC closed its doors.

While the Browns took the NFL by storm, winning the championship their very first year in the league, success took a little longer in coming for the 49ers. They quickly established a reputation as a team with some offensive firepower—but one whose defense didn't always keep pace.

One of the team's stars in the early 1950s was halfback Hugh McElhenny. "The King," as McElhenny was called, had dazzling moves that often left opponents grasping at air when they tried to tackle him. McElhenny, who was the 1952 NFL player of the year, was another future member of the Pro Football Hall of Fame. So was fullback John Henry Johnson, who finished second only to teammate Joe Perry among all NFL players in rushing in 1954.

The 49ers have mostly been known for their quarterbacks, however. And in 1957, they featured a great one in Y.A. Tittle. Tittle—you guessed it, he was a future Hall of Famer, too—took the team to the playoffs for the first time, but the 49ers blew a big lead and lost to Detroit in a showdown for the Western Conference championship.

That team featured players such as R.C. Owens, Bob St. Clair, and Leo Nomellini. Owens was a flanker who perfected the "Alley-Oop" pass with quarterback Y.A. Tittle. Owens, a former college basketball player, would run to the end zone, stop, and leap higher than the defensive backs to catch a high-arcing pass from Tittle. St. Clair was a huge, 6-foot-9 (206 cm) tackle who bulldozed opposing defensive linemen and blocked kicks. Nomellini was a native of Italy who did professional wrestling on the side.

After 1957, no 49ers' team reached the playoffs until 1970. The fans stuck with the team, though, and became known as "The 49er Faithful." When the team finally did make the playoffs again in 1970, it was stopped by the Dallas Cowboys in the final game played at Kezar (the team moved into Candlestick Park, now called Monster Park, in 1971). The Cowboys ended the 49ers' Super Bowl hopes in 1971 and 1972, too.

In a city famous for earthquakes, San Francisco's team didn't even produce a tremor the rest of the 1970s. The 49ers were a miserable 2–14 in both 1978 and 1979. However, two good things happened in 1979: The 49ers hired Bill Walsh as head coach, and Walsh chose quarterback Joe Montana from Notre Dame in the **draft.**

Montana was supposedly too slow, too small, and too weak-armed to make it in the NFL. Doubts

The 1954 49ers featured the "Million-Dollar Backfield"—so named not for the amount of money the players made, but for their amazing talents. The quarterback was Y.A. Tittle, the fullbacks were Joe Perry and John Henry Johnson, and the halfback was Hugh McElhenny. All four players are in the Pro Football Hall of Fame.

Joe Montana's ability to stay calm under pressure helped carry the 49ers to four Super Bowl wins in the 1980s.

remained until December 7, 1980. On that afternoon, the 49ers trailed the New Orleans Saints 35–7 at halftime. Montana took the 49ers on four touchdown drives to tie the score. Ray Wersching's field goal in overtime ended it, 38–35. The 49ers had the greatest regular-season comeback win in NFL history. Montana had arrived.

The 49ers owned the rest of the **decade.** In 1981, they exacted revenge on the Cowboys in the NFC Championship Game. Montana's touchdown pass to Dwight Clark with just 51 seconds left gave San

After years of playing in Joe Montana's shadow, Steve Young emerged as a Hall of Fame quarterback himself.

Francisco a dramatic 28–27 victory. Two weeks later, San Francisco won the Super Bowl for the first time, beating Cincinnati 26–21 in Super Bowl XVI.

In the 1984 season, San Francisco won Super Bowl XIX over the Miami Dolphins, 38–16. Then Jerry Rice arrived, and the 49ers really became dangerous.

Rice was the best wide receiver, if not overall player, ever to grace the NFL. He caught more passes for more yards and more touchdowns than anyone else in history. Rice played 16 seasons in San Francisco (1985–2000).

Montana and Rice teamed up to help the 49ers to another pair of Super Bowl wins. San Francisco beat Cincinnati 20–16 in Super Bowl XXIII to close the 1988 season, then pounded Denver 55–10 the next year.

In all, Montana won four Super Bowls as a starting quarterback. He never threw an interception in the big game and was named Super Bowl MVP a record three times.

In 1991, Steve Young took over as the 49ers' starting quarterback. Young continued San Francisco's run of success. Montana had been league MVP twice. Young also would become a two-time league MVP. Young tossed six touchdown passes while leading the 49ers to the franchise's fifth Super Bowl win, a 49–26 rout of the San Diego Chargers in game XXIX. Only Pittsburgh and Dallas also have won the Super Bowl five times. No team has won it more.

The 49ers haven't been back to the Super Bowl since. Young retired after the 1999 season and Rice left the team following the 2000 season. Although San Francisco did reach the postseason six times in the eight-season span from 1995 to 2002, the proud franchise hit rock bottom in 2004. The 49ers dropped to 2–14, the worst record in the entire league.

Mike Nolan took over as coach in 2005. He is the son of Dick Nolan, the coach who took the 49ers to the playoffs three times in the 1970s. Under Mike Nolan, the 49ers have featured a role reversal: The emphasis has been on improving the

Will Alex Smith become the next great 49ers' quarterback? San Francisco fans sure hope so!

defense, while the offense has not done well. But the offense does feature young stars such as quarterback Alex Smith and running back Frank Gore. Gore set a club record with 1,695 rushing yards in 2006.

Given the 49ers' history, it doesn't figure to be long before they are lighting up scoreboards all around the NFL once again.

CHAPTER FOUR

THE SEATTLE SEAHAWKS

T he Seattle Seahawks are the new kids on the block in the NFC West. While the other teams in the division have histories that date to the 1940s (and before), Seattle did not join the NFL until it began as an **expansion team** in 1976. And, except for that first year, the Seahawks played in the American Football Conference (AFC) until 2002. Since becoming permanent members of the NFC West that season, however, the new kids on the block have turned into the bullies of the division: Seattle won the West for the fourth year in a row in 2007.

One of the Seahawks' division championships, in 2005, led to the club's first Super Bowl berth. Seattle lost that game to the Pittsburgh Steelers, but the season clearly marked the Seahawks' status as one of the best teams in the NFL in the 2000s.

Seattle's ascent to that level started in 1976. The Seahawks made great strides in their early years—much greater than expansion teams usually

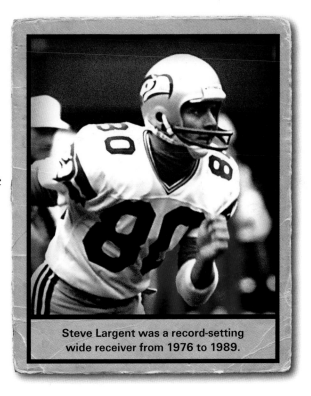

Steve Largent was a record-setting wide receiver from 1976 to 1989.

did back then. Seattle joined the NFL the same season as fellow expansion team Tampa Bay. The Seahawks played their first season as a member of the NFC West, with the understanding that they would shift to the AFC West the following season. They remained in the AFC until the league's latest realignment plan in 2002 shifted them back to the NFC West.

No one expects an expansion team to win a lot of games the first season—and Seattle met expectations. Still, the Seahawks were surprisingly competitive under coach Jack Patera. They almost beat St. Louis in the first game in their franchise history. The Cardinals held on to win 30–24, though, when they intercepted a pass in the end zone on the final play.

Seattle eventually lost its first five games, then defeated the Buccaneers 13–10 on October 17, 1976, for its first victory. That game was called the "Expansion Bowl." The Seahawks won only one more game during their initial season. That victory came when they defeated the Atlanta Falcons 30–13 at home in the Kingdome in front of more than 60,000 rowdy fans.

Seattle was 2–12 that first year, but the club improved quickly. The Seahawks finished 9–7 in 1978, their third season. No third-year expansion team had ever finished with a better record. Quarterback Jim Zorn led the AFC in pass completions (248) and yardage (3,283). Future Pro Football Hall of Fame wide receiver Steve Largent caught 71 passes, also tops in the conference.

Seattle's first win in 1976 came against the Tampa Bay Buccaneers. It was a 13–10 victory. The game was called the "Expansion Bowl" because it pitted the two first-year teams against each other.

In 1976, Jim Zorn was the first starting quarterback in Seahawks' history. Now he's the Redskins' head coach.

Fullback David Sims led the AFC with 15 touchdowns, but was forced to retire the following year due to a neck injury.

The Seahawks made their first great draft pick in 1981, selecting UCLA All-America safety Kenny Easley. Seattle was still too thin on defense, however, and finished in last place in the AFC West for the second straight season.

During the 1982 NFL players' strike, Patera was fired as coach. Patera had been the Seahawks' only coach until then. In 1983, Chuck Knox, who had won six division titles with the Los Angeles Rams and Buffalo Bills in the last decade, became head coach.

Knox was dedicated to establishing a rushing attack in Seattle. His offense became known as "Ground Chuck." Its **cornerstone** was running back Curt Warner from Penn State. Warner had a fantastic rookie season. He led the AFC in rushing with 1,449 yards in 1983, and the Seahawks won nine games while qualifying for the playoffs for the first time ever.

Another new face on offense was Dave Krieg. An unlikely NFL star, Krieg had played at tiny Milton College, a school that no longer even existed. He was efficient and effective, though. In Seattle's first postseason game, Krieg completed 12 of 13 passes for 200 yards and three touchdowns. Seattle wiped out the Broncos 31–7.

Seattle surprised the NFL yet again the following week. Warner rushed for 113 yards as the Seahawks upset the Miami Dolphins 27–20 on the road. Suddenly, the Seahawks found themselves in the AFC Championship Game against the Los Angeles Raiders. The dream ended in southern California. The Raiders won 30–14.

Seattle won its season-opener for the first time in franchise history in 1984. The Seahawks beat the Cleveland Browns 33–0, but paid a huge price for the win. Warner suffered a season-ending knee

The only uniform number that the Seahawks have retired is 12. It's not for any player, though. Instead, it's for the loud fans that give the club a definite home-field advantage. Those fans are collectively called the "12th Man."

From the club's earliest days in the Kingdome up to the present time in Qwest Field, Seattle's fans been among the NFL's most enthusiastic.

injury. Still, Seattle went on to finish 12–4 that year, its best record ever. Easley was named the NFL's defensive player of the year.

Seattle hosted the defending Super Bowl-champion Raiders in a 1984 AFC Wild-Card Playoff Game. The Seahawks won 13–7 in front of the frenzied Kingdome fans. The next weekend, the Seahawks lost at Miami 31–10.

By 1986, Warner was back to his old self. He led the AFC in rushing with a career-high 1,481 yards. Seattle finished 10–6 but in third place in the strong AFC West.

The Seahawks made the playoffs in 1987 and 1988, but met only misery, losing their first game each time.

Running back Shaun Alexander is a touchdown machine. He set a league record (since broken) when he scored 28 times in 2005.

Largent retired in 1989. Not very fast and not 6 feet (183 cm) tall, Largent retired with 819 career catches and with at least one reception in 177 consecutive games. Both were records then, though both have since been broken.

The Seahawks had few highlights in the 1990s. They made the playoffs only once all decade. That came in 1999, when they went 9–7 before losing to Miami in the first round.

The Kingdome, Seattle's only home until then, was demolished following the 1999 season. After playing two seasons at the University of Washington's Husky Stadium, Seattle moved into brand-new Seahawks Stadium (it's called Qwest Field now) in 2002.

On September 29, in front of a national television audience on ESPN, running back Shaun Alexander ran for five touchdowns in the first half against the Vikings. A year earlier, also on an ESPN Sunday-night telecast, Alexander galloped for 266 yards and three touchdowns against the Raiders.

That was just a preview of things to come. In 2004, Alexander rushed for a career-best 1,696 yards and scored 20 touchdowns to help the Seahawks win the NFC West for the first time. It was the third time in the six seasons since Mike Holmgren took over as head coach in 1999 that Seattle had reached the playoffs. But also for the third time, the Seahawks lost in the opening round. A narrow, 27–20 loss to division-rival St. Louis left Seattle still seeking its first postseason victory since the 1984 season.

That win came the following year. First, Alexander set an NFL record by scoring 28 touchdowns as the Seahawks won a club-record 13 games during the regular season. Alexander got lots of help from quarterback Matt Hasselbeck, who passed for 24 touchdowns. Then, Seattle beat Washington 20–10 in an NFC Divisional Playoff Game. The next week, the Seahawks routed Carolina 34–14 in the conference title game to reach the Super Bowl for the first time.

The Pittsburgh Steelers won Super Bowl XL 21–10 in Detroit that year. But the Seahawks believe it was only a temporary detour on their road to an NFL championship.

TIME LINE

1920
Chicago Cardinals become charter members of the NFL

1925
Cardinals are named NFL champions after going 11–2–1

1937
Rams begin play in Cleveland

1960
Chicago Cardinals move to St. Louis

1920   **1930**   **1940**   **1950**   **1960**

1946
San Francisco 49ers are founded as part of the All-America Football Conference (AAFC); Cleveland shifts its franchise to Los Angeles

1947
Cardinals win the NFL Championship Game for the first and, to date, only time

1950
The AAFC folds, but the 49ers join the NFL

1951
Los Angeles Rams win their first league championship

1994
49ers beat San Diego in game XXIX for their fifth Super Bowl victory

1988
Cardinals move to Phoenix (they'll become known as the Arizona Cardinals in 1994)

1995
Los Angeles Rams move to St. Louis

1981
San Francisco wins the first of four Super Bowls in the 1980s

1999
Rams win Super Bowl XXXIV, their first NFL title in 48 years

1970 **1980** **1990** **2000** **2010**

2004
Seahawks win the NFC West for the first time

2005
Seattle reaches the Super Bowl for the first time, but loses game XL to the Pittsburgh Steelers

1976
Seattle Seahawks join the NFL as an expansion team

2007
Seahawks win the NFC West for the fourth year in a row

STAT STUFF

TEAM RECORDS (THROUGH 2007)*

Team	All-time Record	Number of Titles (Most Recent)	Number of Times in Playoffs	Top Coach (Wins)
Arizona	466–672–39	2 (1947)	7	Don Coryell (42)
St. Louis	520–478–20	3 (1999)	27	John Robinson (79)
San Francisco	475–396–13	5 (1994)	22	George Seifert (108)
Seattle	253–264–0	0	10	Mike Holmgren (86)

*includes NFL totals only

NFC WEST CAREER LEADERS (THROUGH 2007)

Category	Name (Years With Team)	Total
Arizona		
Rushing yards	Ottis Anderson (1979–1986)	7,999
Passing yards	Jim Hart (1966–1983)	34,639
Touchdown passes	Jim Hart (1966–1983)	209
Receptions	Larry Centers (1990–98)	535
Touchdowns	Roy Green (1979–1990)	70
Scoring	Jim Bakken (1962–1978)	1,380
St. Louis		
Rushing yards	Eric Dickerson (1983–87)	7,245
Passing yards	Jim Everett (1986–1993)	23,758
Touchdown passes	Roman Gabriel (1962–1972)	154
Receptions	Isaac Bruce (1994–2007)	942
Touchdowns	Marshall Faulk (1999–2005)	85
Scoring	Jeff Wilkins (1997–2004)	1,223
San Francisco		
Rushing yards	Joe Perry (1950–1960, 1963)	7,344
Passing yards	Joe Montana (1979–1992)	35,124
Touchdown passes	Joe Montana (1979–1992)	244
Receptions	Jerry Rice (1985–2000)	1,281
Touchdowns	Jerry Rice (1985–2000)	187
Scoring	Jerry Rice (1985–2000)	1,130
Seattle		
Rushing yards	Shaun Alexander (2000–07)	9,429
Passing yards	Dave Krieg (1980–1991)	26,132
Touchdown passes	Dave Krieg (1980–1991)	195
Receptions	Steve Largent (1976–1989)	819
Touchdowns	Shaun Alexander (2000–07)	112
Scoring	Norm Johnson (1982–1990)	810

MEMBERS OF THE PRO FOOTBALL HALL OF FAME

Player	Position	Date Inducted
Arizona		
Charles W. Bidwill Sr.	Owner	1967
Guy Chamberlin	End	1965
Jimmy Conzelman	Quarterback	1964
Dan Dierdorf	Tackle	1996
John "Paddy" Driscoll	Quarterback	1965
Walt Kiesling	Guard/Coach	1966
Earl "Curly" Lambeau	Coach	1963
Dick "Night Train" Lane	Cornerback	1974
Ollie Matson	Halfback	1972
Don Maynard	Wide Receiver	1987
Ernie Nevers	Fullback	1963
Jackie Smith	Tight End	1994
Jim Thorpe	Halfback	1963
Charley Trippi	Halfback/Quarterback	1968
Roger Wehrli	Cornerback	2007
Larry Wilson	Safety	1978
St. Louis		
George Allen	Coach	2002
Bob "Boomer" Brown	Tackle	2004
Eric Dickerson	Running Back	1999
Tom Fears	End	1970
Bill George	Linebacker	1974
Sid Gillman	Coach	1983
Elroy "Crazylegs" Hirsch	Halfback/End	1968
David "Deacon" Jones	Defensive End	1980
Dick "Night Train" Lane	Cornerback	1974
James Lofton	Wide Receiver	2003
Tom Mack	Guard	1999
Ollie Matson	Halfback	1972
Tommy McDonald	Wide Receiver	1998
Joe Namath	Quarterback	1985
Merlin Olsen	Defensive Tackle	1982
Dan Reeves	Owner	1967
Andy Robustelli	Defensive End	1971
Texas E. "Tex" Schramm	President/General Manager	1991
Jackie Slater	Tackle	2001
Norm Van Brocklin	Quarterback	1971
Bob Waterfield	Quarterback	1965
Ron Yary	Tackle	2001
Jack Youngblood	Defensive End	2001

MORE STAT STUFF

MEMBERS OF THE PRO FOOTBALL HALL OF FAME

Player	Position	Date Inducted
San Francisco		
Fred Dean	Defensive End	2008
Jimmy Johnson	Cornerback	1994
John Henry Johnson	Fullback	1987
Ronnie Lott	Cornerback/Safety	2000
Hugh McElhenny	Halfback	1970
Joe Montana	Quarterback	2002
Leo Nomellini	Defensive Tackle	1969
Joe Perry	Fullback	1969
Bob St. Clair	Tackle	1990
O.J. Simpson	Running Back	1985
Y.A. Tittle	Quarterback	1971
Bill Walsh	Coach	1993
Dave Wilcox	Linebacker	2000
Steve Young	Quarterback	2005
Seattle		
Carl Eller	Defensive End	2004
Franco Harris	Running Back	1990
Steve Largent	Wide Receiver	1995
Warren Moon	Quarterback	2006

Bill Walsh coached the 49ers to three Super Bowl wins.

GLOSSARY

consecutive—in a row

contract—an agreement to do something (in this case, play football for the team)

cornerstone—a very important part of something

decade—any 10-year period, such as the 1980s

draft—held each April, this is when NFL teams choose college players to join their teams; teams with the worst records the prior year choose first, but draft picks can be traded to move a team's draft order

dynasty—a group or team that is successful for a long period of time

era—period of time

expansion team—a new franchise that starts from scratch

franchise—more than just the team, it is the entire organization that is a member of a professional sports league

Heisman Trophy—the award given each year to the best player in college football

integrate—to give all races an opportunity to belong

migrate—to move from one region to another

playoffs—after the regular schedule, these are the games played to determine the champion

postseason—the period in which the playoffs are held

Pro Bowl—the NFL's all-star game

professional—someone who is paid to perform an activity (in this case, play football)

realignment—a change in the way something is organized

rivalry—when people (or teams) compete for the same goal

rookie—an athlete in his or her first season as a professional

successor—someone who follows someone else in an order

Super Bowl—the NFL's annual championship game, played in late January or early February at a different stadium each year

tandems—two parts working together

veteran—a player who is experienced from many seasons in the league

wild-card—a team that makes the playoffs without winning a division title

FIND OUT MORE

Books

Bell, Lonnie. *The History of the St. Louis Rams*. Mankato, Minn.: Creative Education, 2004.

Bell, Lonnie. *The History of the San Francisco 49ers*. Mankato, Minn.: Creative Education, 2005.

Buckley, James Jr. *Eyewitness Super Bowl*. New York: DK Publishing, 2003.

Frederick, Sara, and Sara Gilbert. *The History of the Arizona Cardinals*. Mankato, Minn.: Creative Education, 2005.

Frederick, Sara, and Sara Gilbert. *The History of the Seattle Seahawks*. Mankato, Minn.: Creative Education, 2005.

Ladewski, Paul. *National Football League Superstars 2007*. New York: Scholastic, 2007.

Preller, James. *Super Bowl Super Quarterbacks*. New York: Scholastic, 2005.

On the Web

Visit our Web site for lots of links about the NFC West: *http://www.childsworld.com/links*

Note to Parents, Teachers, and Librarians: We routinely verify our Web links to make sure they are safe, active sites—so encourage your readers to check them out!

INDEX